Hops Hill School had a new computer.

"You can get a new pen-pal on the computer," said Miss Mills.

Sam had a go on the computer.
"I am Sam. I go to Hops Hill School," he wrote.

"Hello, Sam. I am Charlie," wrote Charlie on the computer. "I go to Five Lanes School."

Then Charlie wrote, "Five Lanes School is the best at football."

"Oh no, you're not!" wrote Sam.
"Oh yes, we are!" wrote Charlie.

Ravi ran in.

He had the list for the big football match.

Football Matches for May

May 12th
Digton School
vs
All Bells School

May 14th
Catwell School
vs
Old Hall School

May 16th
Five Lanes School
vs
Hops Hill School

The list said that Hops Hill School was going to play Five Lanes School!

It was the day of the big football match.

Five Lanes School had the ball.

"Chip it over to Charlie," said Five Lanes School.
"Chip it over to Charlie!"

"Are you Charlie?" said Sam.

"Yes," said Charlie, "and Five Lanes School is the best!"

"Oh no, you're not," said Ravi. He got the ball.

Sam ran with the ball.

He shot into the net.

"Hops Hill School is the best!" said Sam.